AFTER MIDNIGHT

After Midnight

Selected Poems

Joseph Bobrow

il piccolo editions
by
fisher king press

il piccolo editions, an imprint of Fisher King Enterprises LLC
www.fisherkingpress.com
info@fisherkingpress.com
+1-307-222-9575

After Midnight: Selected Poems
Copyright © 2017 Joseph Bobrow
ISBN 978-1-77169-042-3 Paperback
ISBN 978-1-77169-043-0 eBook
First Edition

For Joseph Caston

Contents

That I Cannot Do

"That I cannot do,"
the Godfather said to Bonasera, when the undertaker asked
for justice on the day Sicilian fathers
entertain such requests.
"Your daughter is still alive"
said Don Corleone.
The undertaker's whispers asked for murder,
Measure is needed even
when dispensing
vengeance

I would if I could
if I had the power of life and death
like the suits

I would prevent harm from coming to David:
Colonel, social worker, father, comrade-
in-arms of peace and healing.
I would protect him and the soldier-therapists,
chaplains, and mental health
techs under his command
Women, men, seasoned hands and newbies
All headed into the hornets nest
we sat, spoke and listened
in stillness
felt the energy of sanctuary
looked each other in the eye

I would if I could
protect and watch over them
like a good father
a godfather
heavenly father
I am not
though my impact is not
inconsequential

I would keep them safe keep them alive,
feel your weight on the chair, sink in, soft belly
rises and falls,
we practice meditation together
after ten minutes I suggest
they shift their attention back
but no one moves
nary a whisper
jumping jacks leaping up for refills of coffee
  are all still
out of the quiet depth they speak
one by one
they speak of their families
the ache of separation: "My mom is sick; who will care
for her?" "I'll miss my first baby's birth. Will she know me
when I return?"
  If   I return

jacks in the box
we all sit together
counting our breaths
stopping looking, listening,
recognizing, remembering and returning

to body and breath, flesh and blood, here and now
we wish safety equanimity
strength and peace of mind to loved ones, to all of us,
to ourselves
and no one wants to stop

they say pre-deployment everyone's so
toughened up
but rest, energy, silent closeness,
peace and life are flowing here still
and sure

L'chaim
To life

maybe they don't want it to end
because they know
and they don't know
what is
to come

David calls a break, has to leave early
to prepare for an IED detection field exercise
I know he is leaving
for nine months
enough time for a baby
we hug unabashedly
I cradle his head against my chest
he points to the little Buddha I gave him, tucked inside the
chest pocket
of his cammies
I still don't get it until he says "love ya,"
that's what I whispered in his ear at my place

when his friends sent him off,
I get it
he is saying goodbye

L'chaim
To life

I would if I could
heal and protect,
it happens, you know
mysterious energy
like a shaman
I could do it, maybe
but do I want to take it all on? make it mine?
their fate?

I see each one of them in my mind's eye
their beauty, noble and fragile
I let them flow in me
and then, like them,
I get on with it

Passing over the Cascades then Shasta
on the return
the tears come

I would if I could,
if I had the power of the suits, the
power of life and death over
young lives

That I cannot do

"But, if some unlucky accident should befall him, if he
should get shot in the head by a police officer, or hang
himself in his jail cell, or if he's struck by a bolt of lightning
— then I'm going to blame some of the people in this room,
and that I do not forgive," said Don Corleone.

Should something befall David
grief washes over me now
I know
of course
the awful possibility

I can only imagine my helpless rage

this senseless war

Meeting the Unspeakable

We watch, we hear, we feel,
Do we? The impacts. Japan.

> "The epicenter of the earthquake that devastated north-
> ern Japan was just off the islands of Matsushima. A coast-
> al wonderland, dotted with jutting rocks and stunningly
> beautiful islands, it had been the chosen home of Basho
> in the later years of his life."

Ah, Matsushima!
Ah-ah Matsushima!
Ah! Matsushima! Ah!

Basho gives us Matsushima. It helps me bear the unbearable.

I write some friends, placing his poem at the end of each
message:

"Filled with grief at the devastation in Japan that ripples
through us all. A sangha member reminded me of Basho's
poem. Thank God for poetry."

One friend, a Japanese Zen master, writes back,

"Thank you for your concern. Seeing the earthquake and tsu-
nami and nuclear plant, it is evident Buddha nature is beyond
our thought and emotions. When we grasp earthquake and
tsunami and nuclear plant we and they together become
Buddha nature. In that moment, Buddha nature is activated.
In the Matsushima islands, new seasons will come and go."

I respond:

The earth shakes
the ground buckles
the seas heave
screams of people and animals
the spinach is poisoned
who raises the concept of Buddha Nature?
emerge from your cave
How do you respond?

Him:

You are concerning deeply.
Anyway, making one more person who understands
Buddha nature deeply is the most important work for priests.

Me:

The power of
our Buddha nature
is that
there is no
such thing
as Buddha nature,
It springs forth
laughing and weeping,
now beautiful
now disastrous,
Realizing this
let us cherish and protect
all beings

our original flesh and blood,
respond in
accord with circumstances, and
save all beings
Ha!
already realized, they
need no saving
nothing to save
so
we vow
to save them

Him:

Your poem is very nice. Even though it is an abstract way
of writing I can visualize it, almost see it, with natural scenic
illustrations. Today I am going to prepare our garden to plant
potatoes.

How will you meet the unspeakable?

Today I Heard the Seals Again

Walking my favorite path,
Land's End,
where the land ends
on the bluff, northwest edge of San Francisco
Marin headlands golden across the bay to the north
Golden Gate to the east,
vast and shimmering the Pacific to the west,
bright, hot summer day, smells strong and full, flowers
everywhere, like so many summer days
in New York.
faintly, in the distance, I hear it,
like a mirage
then again, around a bend,
      Arp! Arp! Arp!
flood of emotion courses through cells
they were lured away from Seal Rock to Pier 39
used to hear them every day as I
washed the dishes,
in the evening as I drifted into sleep
wild
after so long, they're back
now, yet before,
before the partings, losses, and cruelty
      Arp!   Arp!
I shake with emotion, joy and pain cascading in
My son is leaving.
Spread your wings and fly free.
In one moment, the wild

freedom bursts through:

       Arp! Arp! Arp!

The pure sunshine of your smiling face,
the joy of being alive, together,   wild.
Before, Now, On your way

Day of Atonement

In a moment of forgetting, gazing at a photo of a soldier on
a book cover, it comes to me:

I'm born of brokenness and damage

He was my father but I didn't know him.
driven by the blind struggle to forget, maybe to heal
he took a shortcut to redemption

"I did some things during the war."

I glean a few details here and there, across the decades,
like scattered dispatches from the front,
thirty years after his death
his daughter says
he never spoke about it
my mother too, he never spoke to her

may have killed people
feet froze, almost amputated
surgery in England
Lost his father suddenly, age four
one brother during, one right after
the   war
Where did the men go?

He had a wife, a six year old daughter

"I did some things during the war."
"I wasn't proud of"
"I couldn't go back."

Threw himself into "The Cause"

empower the disenfranchised workers
Swept up in the fight for justice
and the thrill of making the revolution,
he threw himself into   my mother

I wanted to know
my creation story.
"How old was I? Six months? A year?"
her accounts change;
memory and inclination are subject
to conditions on the ground.
He left, that's it
"I wanted to take you with me," he says much later,
the year he died.

*****

A young man, I'm reweaving the threads
working with the thinnest of yarns
I know so little

The holocaust as mini-series on TV
with Meryl Streep
I wept all night.
Years pass and the show is on again

"Come watch Dad, it's powerful."
"I've seen too much," he says.

I met him at 24
when we hugged the first time in Venice California he
almost squeezed the air out of me.

In the valley of Saint Fernando, on Noble Avenue
when there were still 2 acre plots

we repaired the fences, pounded nails, smell of cedar planks,
sweating alongside him, whew
  the joy
I laid large pieces of red tile in the ground outside the sliding doors
collected black walnuts on the ground, from big trees, mixed in
with piles of leaves
some were rotten,
apricot, orange, cherry, tangerine, apple trees
some fragrant with blossoms, some heavy with fruit.

*****

He develops this hacking cough
it's the smoking, he says, but he doesn't stop
he's puffing away as we drive to his medical appointment
I'm pissed
I want as much of him as I can get,
he ignores his health as he ignored his son
and the wounds of war
rippling silently through heart and soul.

The cough gets worse, pneumonia he says, but when I finally get up
the gumption to confront him
— no more of this honeymoon business —
he owns up: it's leukemia.

I thought I had all the time in the world
to repair and reconnect, but no
his condition worsens, four years after we met, his doctor calls
"Come now, if you want to see him again."
I leave Boston, spend three months with him
in his LA hospital room.

One day as I arrive at the hospital he's marching madly
down the hall, flailing about
dragging the I.V. bag on the ground behind him
gown all undone, needle still in his arm,
he's screaming
"They want to kill me"
yes

Nurses desperate rush when they see me, "he's asking for you"
like a Commander calling "Medic! Soldier down!"
but it's not just anyone he wants; it's me
I get him back to his room, we wash off the blood and
change his clothes. He lays down and tells me
"I want to go home." Back to the cherry and apricot trees.
But his wife and his substitute doctor say no
I don't have the say
so I'm just his son.

*****

Twenty five years later I ask
"Why am I throwing myself
into working with warriors and families?"
"Why have I caught this passion?"
Helping them knit themselves back together,
build new heart tissue,
reweave broken narrative materiel,
Am I repairing my dad? Healing myself?
maybe, not quite, not completely

Born of damage, the brokenness of war,
a man's search to hold together,

to keep from unraveling

"He was the life of the party, he played the piano, he
sang show tunes, he was
handsome, he was 'Everything I Wanted,'"
says my mother, now 95

I glimpse her love for him every once in a great while.
Once over coffee at Mel's Diner on Geary, at 85, she says
"You look like Bob now, the look you have."
my father enters my mother
from left field,
this time it's a blessing
  their love is palpable
and my mother's eyes grow watery as she describes the look she saw
on my face; his look, on my face

We are what we make of the cards we're dealt
they made me

Did the passion bind his wounds, knit him together?
was there tenderness? love?
"The Cause" was the gasoline
was lust the spark?
so strong, it made an anxious woman "Risk Everything."
  they risked it all: marriages, daughters, husband, wife,
their son-to-be

I see myself at five:
I'm throwing my pink ball against the wall,
catch a la solitaire,
other kids have dads.
 a dark cloud trailing
envelops me in loneliness
  I didn't know how much

I didn't know
about him, about my beginnings

Don't get me wrong
I'm glad to be here
grateful for this life
it's just that
coming into this world
this way
filled me with shame
I helped so many with theirs,
shame was foreign to me

  a boy feels like a foreigner without his father

*****

I see him now, as I gaze into the face of the grizzled soldier,
a man's face, features ruddy and rugged,
I remember, on this Day of Atonement:
  the image from *Life* magazine
is one he liked

a photo   journalist
he knew good pictures when he saw them,
liked them black and white, gritty and earthy

but being drawn to this image
is not a matter of aesthetics.
Something resonates, something missing
in the eyes of the soldier. His eyes say "Vacancy,"
vacate the premises

I'm up at night, heartbeats out of whack,
What is this? Moan? Muffled sob? Strangled cry? Suffocated scream?

Cri de coeur
Ocean of tears
I can barely form the word: daddy

*****

Steve, first one I told
he's ex-Army, former Ranger, injured face and hands in explosion
in Desert Storm
different fathers, different wars, same story
American troops make babies with Vietnamese
women, but hell, that's just the tip of the iceberg.
I see now; we're comrades in brokenness
we go way   back
children born of war's damage
my shame ebbs;
I have plenty of company

They did some things in the war
They saw too much
horrors that hurtled them
toward passion
and a hidden wish: turn death into life

But oh   the wreckage
   collateral damage, we
kids try to layer back unraveled threads of connective tissue
repair unseen wounds

light enters now, through the breakage
illuminating all of war's casualties
it's not just US – but birds and fishes, air and water and earth,
generations
unborn

17

*****

I come to the hospital, but he's not in his room.
He's in a renal coma, for Christ sakes, how far can he get?
I search everywhere
finally find him in Med-Surg: emergency peritoneal dialysis.

I push past the nursing staff, shouts louder and louder, "No,
you can't go in there!" I open the door to the operating room

There he is, his body racked by spasms, coughing fits lift him
off the table, blood all over

so much for the blessings of renal failure, a peaceful death
so much for Do No Harm
heroes united in combating
the arch enemy of death.
I vow not to return.

Next day I spend the morning with Lizzie,
my new seven year-old niece, while Suzy,
my new older sister, takes the 405 slog into LA to Kaiser

Returning from the zoo, Lizzy crashes.
I lay down in another room
afternoon sun hot, bright
I doze off and begin falling tumbling down a long tunnel
at the bottom of the tunnel
clear as day

there he is

sitting up cross-legged in his hospital bed,
distended Buddha belly,
gown up around his thighs.

I begin to speak,
walk him through the last moments,

as I did two weeks ago
when his breath got raspy and crackly, like a death-rattle

"you can let go, it's okay," I say

He laughs and says "Buddhism schmuddhism;
I just want you to know
how much it means that you came,
that you're here with me"

And we hug.

Basking, I slowly begin the return back up the tunnel,
When I arrive I try to open my eyes, but I can't.
I'm alert but I can't feel any sensation.
I've forgotten where I am, and what I was doing.
When I try to move, I can't.
Must be half hour later, I'm able to move a finger, then a hand
I get up,
shaky, awestruck, full

That night cleaning the kitchen
I see a cockroach crawling slowly along the linoleum
near the garbage cabinet
under the sink.
I watch as it moves, slower and slower;
then it stops.

the visible and invisible worlds are
both speaking goodbye

The next morning I get a call
when I arrive he's gone

Vacated the premises

It's Father's Day, 1979

I have become his son, and he, my father.

my passionate flawed warrior dad
   we found each other
   by the bedside,
   in the walnut groves,
   in my mother's eyes,
   in the language
   between worlds

now I wish you
   "the wideness, the foolish loving spaces
   full of heart."[1]

---

1 Gary Snyder, *Mountains and Rivers Without End* (Washington DC: Counterpoint, 1996), 152.

Play

Lichen lei   play
smiles light up the forest
presence of bear
scent of ginseng
deep moistness
tracks of mountain lion
owl's hoot
crows' sky dance
Dance of
          Ideas   sparks

Bouncing with excitement
Look! what I found!

Howls of delight
bubble up from lovemaking
          jouissance
Tunes, dreams, crazy verses
Sweaty love in fire's hot glow
Juices flowing, intermingling
Starfish, mussels, pelicans, osprey,
seals, surf and clouds

Laughter – Laughter –
running on the beach like kids

resting now
on a dune, sweet drift
between the currents

After Midnight

Thirty seven years ago
on a sunny cloudless day
sitting zazenkai with meditation comrades
in the redwood living room dojo at 220
between periods I exit to pee
in the outdoor toilets
walking back, I glance in the grass and find our cat,
Madame, black with white markings,
lying there, face convulsed,
lifeless
I bring her to town for an autopsy
drive by Ho'okipa, waves glassy
sun bright, sky clear, trades soft
and it hits me,
our beloved cat dead wrapped in the car
palpable sadness of loss
and, the splendor of something without beginning and end,
going on going on,
I hold this as I enter the vet's office, return with the news that she
was poisoned, probably by a rancher.
I dig a hole in the garden under an avocado tree, wrap her,
gently place her in,
chant the heart sutra, and cover her with dirt.

✳✳✳✳✳

Today, I'm driving west on Geary toward Ocean Beach,
grey clouds part to let through the sun's last rays, bright
next to me, in my car, my beloved Midnight,
black with white markings,

faithful companion for seventeen years,
nearly a third of my life
just got the news: inoperable cancer.
I get her home, she's hyper and ravenous from surgery
I hold her, she settles
slowly she begins to stretch like the cat yogi she is,
we pass the cat's eye marble between us
on the wooden floor, her paws more
nimble than my finger flicks, learned on Bronx streets.

once she took a month-long
walkabout hunting insects
  I found her, my inside cat,
lost, hungry and emaciated
shivering in the mud
in the crawl space under a nearby house.
  the brightness of her yellow eyes returned

now she cradles herself next to me, tight and close
  she rests, she is alive. She is dying. She is alive, She is dying.
I can't imagine her not being here with me
she is here with me.

*****

Tonight, lying in bed
Valentines weekend
my love and I a warm tangle of arms and legs
she on one shoulder, Midnight nestled in on the other
Life's tender mercies all around
Flood of tears
Waves of love and gratitude

Life here, death here,
No life and no death
Love spanning
sadness and loss
        Fullness
spanning life and death
no birth and no death, no beginning and no end,
waves of tears, waves of passion,
crossing to the other shore
this shore, what shore,
waves and water and shore

drops of sorrow without measure

*****

Now it's about a year later
I miss you desperately
I hear a sound, I see a movement, and
there you are
but not
I think it must be the one year
anniversary, no last
year at this time
I thought you were healing, thought
we'd trumped the experts
the day preparing to put you down I asked, a child not knowing
am I doing the right thing?
my lover came up to be here
when the cancer pushed up into
your brain
and you were
no longer

yourself
she stayed in bed held you when I went
talking Zen
you lay on her lap
under the comforter
while she wrote abstract things that didn't make sense
but Midnight's Dream was
the title
I didn't know what to do I didn't want to move
your lifeless body now
in my hands
on the couch
I held you for a long time, then
we put you on the altar, wrapped in fabric
lit the candle burned incense, sat and chanted
later with you in my backpack,
we took candle, incense, matches, shovel
and walked out
at dusk
into the rain
Land's End
darkening sky
the ground was too hard for a hole
in the spot I'd planned for you
so I dug nearby, under a big cypress
and placed you there
covered you with dark earth, cypress needles and grey clay from
deep down
overlooking the
headlands
in the drizzle
I chanted and spoke to the four directions, intoned to the
spirits to welcome us
to welcome you

a voice that came
from where I knew not
a voice of vast love and unspeakable grief
helpless boundless
love
and pain
(I wrote "bondless")
one voice
Gate Gate Paragate Parasam Gate
the rain and the tears

*****

You Must Believe in Spring is playing
  no, it's not the
one year anniversary,
it's the season of your birth
my Midnight
mid
midster
the middle way
the time you were born
eighteen years ago
how I miss you
my dear girl
tears and snot I miss you

  your shiny black coat, the sparkle of
  your yellow eyes

your warm
sustaining
unquestioning
love

Approach

Swimming at Miramar

wings glide inches above

the waves

ah, Pelican

Preponderance of the Small

I removed the lamps from the frames of the paintings
the ones that trailed electrical cord to the outlets
I moved the Chinese watercolor print, swapped places with
Les Raboteurs de Parquet
cleaned off the memorabilia on that odd shelf in the dining room
and put it above the fireplace mantle,
it looks better
oh, and I had the fireplace cleaned
turned out it wasn't backed up
that night
when after evenings of sweaty love
smoke filled the house
the flu couldn't handle the load of smoke
I sold your dresser
but kept the rosewood chair in the bedroom where
it looked surprisingly nice
then I moved it back to the living room where
it fits now that I bought a
big lovely Persian rug
a spare firm oak chair does just fine in the bedroom
You were right about most of the
Small things
I now use citradish for dishes citrawash for clothes and
citrasolv for everything else
I like them
but I'm letting my toenails grow
couldn't tend to them as you did in the bath
and cutting them too close gave me ingrown toenails
had the big harmless cyst removed
but my back is still hairy
I wash my hands a bit more often

clip my nose hairs a bit more frequently
and comb my hair back occasionally
I figured out you liked that because it covered my bald spot better
but I do it anyway
rinsing my hair every day does
the same thing
got the shower fixed
strong steady stream now
and hot and cold blend
haven't gotten my teeth whitened
so I look 10 years younger
like you did
got me one of those eagle creek toiletry bags with all
the compartments
I enjoy packing now
it's an art, and it works,
don't eat kale anymore
can't fathom how paranoid you were
stepping quickly across the hallway into the bedroom
from the shower
in a white towel
as if the neighbors up on the hill
were waiting, peering through the window
with a powerful telescope, at just the precise angle to
catch you in that very moment
I don't fuss with dust and microbes the way you did
the curtains you threw at me and ruined
by advising me to wash them
and then said
they look pretty good
are still there
a pale blue grey would pick up like colors in the new rug
but I prefer the kind that roll down from the top and let
in the light

oh, I got a new bed
it doesn't squeak
it's beautiful
solid wood, Japanese style
two tatamis fit snugly in the frame
sleeping on wood and reeds
and a soft firm mattress
you would like it
but you're not in it
it's mine
I'm here

I thought it was the Kinks but
it's actually
the Zombies
Please don't bother trying to find her
She's not there

gained back the 25 pounds I lost
emptying my bowels again
feel good in my skin

I am here
breathing freely
I belong to the world

New Moon New Love

Driving home after
dinner with my sister Rosy,
happy heart stirring,
rhythms of a new love song become audible
"I can feel your heart," she says during a pause
in conversation. My viscera go
"Ah," and we confess what is palpable.
  now I come to the crest of the sand dune
called Geary Boulevard
and before me is a great big new moon
no a bit bigger than new
 there, hanging in the clear sky
I begin to turn onto 35th Ave as usual
But veer back
and continue on toward
Ocean Beach
come down past the lookout above the
Sutro Baths
the caves and blowholes below, old haunts
for me and my son
past the big curve in the road where the
coastline appears in one fell
swoop, whoosh
I continue down, pull up and park
facing the ocean
we used to boogie board here
I'm listening to Santana
lyrical melodies build slowly to ecstatic riffs

I watch the moon glowing

then I leave the car and walk out onto the beach

head for the shadows, where the street light does not reach

and keep going, down to the shoreline

Moon ripples on the water, waves luminescent

flocks of barely visible sandpipers flutter

like sea bubbles

silently

there's a fire under an overhang on the steeply sloping retaining

wall my son and I used to climb

Stars brilliant

Moon lit by sun's fire

even the part that's dark,

   Incandescent

I stand, as the tide comes in, and the spindly legged birds move

as one

Dream

For Joe Caston on his 80th birthday

They come unbidden in sleep
unspool and spin together,
intrigue, inform, and surprise

they wake us
up shake
us up

arrive in
daytime
lure us away

they harbor wishes and knowledge
unclaimed

live through us like
unspoken expectations
of tribe family and culture
ours but not ours, a
case of mistaken identity;
we shake free
Dream is
  magic
young boys in Black Orpheus they race
to the favela hilltop
guitar in hand just in time
to sing the sun up—
the ancient myth lives anew

wake up, nothing
comes to a sleeper
but a dream.
analysts say au contraire
don't mess with the unfolding drama
make it make sense
or ask
if the teddy was found or made
up, real or unreal
      do not disturb

it is dream that animates
what we create
in our wake
as we go about
our nights and days

when our loved one dies, she is gone yet
here here yet gone
mystery
to be lived, unsolved

we know dreams
wake us up we know
they keep us asleep and
whole we know daydreams take us far
away
      but

we   wake   dream
bring it
to life

What dream courses through you?

I come from a good dream:
liberation and equality, justice
and peace
from each
according to his abilities to
each according to his needs—
my mother and father's dream
what a thrill to have dreamt it
in solidarity with so many
what a passion play for them to realize and put flesh
to it
(that would be me)
        I dream it today
disseminate it
a new

Buddhists say self is a dream, evanescent
like a cloud
but don't mistake it for nothing
or take it for Maya
listen to Yun-Men,
fierce old Chinese master who
knew nothing
of development, nothing
of the talking cure:
"There must be a person in there!" he roared
twelve hundred years ago,
"Don't just mimic words and phrases."

the true person of no-rank
comes forth

vigorous and distinctive
walks
the dog, looks
for the keys, laughs
and weeps

"ruggedly singular" and ever-changing
at once ineffable and palpable
durable and fragile
"light like a feather, heavy as lead"

Ah, indispensable dreaming!
but
what if
dream itself is how we are
made how we play
the stuff we are made
of how we render each
                other   make
the world

as death is mystery so does living proceed
ungraspable formless form wondrous alchemy

not by discrete steps alone
imagining and implementing, coalescing
and dissolving, but
all together now in round,
        Row row row your boat
        gently down the stream
        merrily merrily
        not always merrily
                        dream

Rela

     sun

        ship   – for Aaron

my son makes art, he is negotiating with a gallerist,
"it's like a relationship, dad."
relay son ship
rela tion shit
roulez son ship
roulez les bons temps
relay sun ship
reallay son ship?
inflated
wor ship
deflated war ship
can someone really love me?
son ship
have my best interests at heart?
sun ship
or am I just an extension?
some shit
a vehicle for their inflation?
oh shit
roulez their bons temps
what does it look like, sound like, feel like
no shit
when someone loves me

sheeit
wants more of me
roulette what the shit
relay sees me as I am
sion ship
rather than through the prism of their
some shit
sans needing me to be
hot shit
how does it affect me?
on a
          cellular level?
Relay   my ship?
son of a ship
scion ship
sometrip
sun

The First Casualties

The first casualties
are thinking, feeling and being
dreaming, imagining, laughing, and crying.

September 11 was an endless loop
a visual blur of pain,
then the announcer stopped,
recited the names of the dead.
one by one
they came to life.

Benumbed or caught up in ill-will
How can we understand when we can't stand?
How can we respond, when response ability is in such short supply?

Monomaniacal thinking hijacks religion
turns it into ideology
the person vanishes
Have I got an idea for you:
            It's to die for
A romance with death.
The precious other
thou
so necessary to think, feel and be,
is sacrificed at the altar of absolute purity

You infect me and mine - I expel you
rid the world of impurity

pernicious sameness reigns supreme
you strike at me, I eradicate you, "evil-doer"
and the beat goes on
tragic misrecognition breeds action that is
sticky
it pulls irresistibly for like-minded reaction
You know how easy it is
we get sucked in.

A teenager once whispered:
"I wish I had the balls of those kids at Columbine."
His father deserted him, he can't grieve and glorifies rage
"Ya feel me?" he asks.
I say:
Maybe it takes real balls not to go off in blind rage -
to stop, look and listen.
Maybe the person next to you can help.
Where is the fertile, durable other?

Respond with love, not might, I hear,
   Ugh
What a force love is when founded in standing
and understanding
and bearing the impossible.
It takes all our power to stop, look and listen,

to protect and nourish and share
the gift of response ability

Mother

May the spirits watch over you
as you make your passage
through unknown lands
May they protect and
shepherd you through
climes that frighten you,
Gone gone gone beyond
But not yet, not yet
      This is the long goodbye
Slow and painful, tender and intimate
        goodbye

In an old Zen story, Changsha is wandering in the mountains.
"Where have you been wandering?" the head monk asked him.

"First I went following the scented grasses; then I returned
following the falling blossoms."

First we went walking at Tennessee Valley, spotted an owl,
high in the eucalyptus.

Then we sauntered across flowering dunes at Fort Funston,
down to the beach below. It was your birthday.

      May beauty surround you

We strolled at Ocean Beach, more slowly as you aged, and your
knees hurt.

I would park and turn off the motor, you would breathe deep and say, "Ah, it's so good to be here."

This is the long goodbye.

Sometimes you would say, "When I go, I'd like to be able to say, 'bye bye,'" "just toodle-loo."

Toodle-loo: "Archaic American form of 'goodbye'. Derives from the French, 'a tout a l'heure,' meaning 'see you later.' Came into vogue after the second world war."

"A toute a l'heure, Maman." I *am* seeing you later, now. A later kind of love, the long toodle-loo, what a treasure.

You would leave so often

Now that I finally have you, you're leaving; so soon?

It's so short, the long goodbye.

Dawn at Paliku

Standing in the meadow

outside the cabin

doing qigong

silence infuses all things

Moon and Jupiter above

first light rising

A single nene circles, tracing the perimeter of the meadow

softly cries

fellow campers in tents still sleeping

breathe in, lead with wrist, arms rise

breathe out, let wrist lead again, arms come down

to earth

Flood of tears and sobs

Now the nene swoops low

a few feet above

my head

Morning benediction

Sun glow builds

wisps of pink clouds fill

the sky

Luminosity touching

    each pu'u

    each mountain ridge

Then it comes to me

We live

in beauty

tears moisten the ancient cinders

About the Author

Joseph Bobrow is the author of *Waking Up From War: A Better Way Home For Veterans And Nations* (foreword by His Holiness the Dalai Lama), *Zen And Psychotherapy: Partners in Liberation* (comments by Ven. Thich Nhat Hanh), and the co-translator of Thich Nhat Hanh's *Guide To Walking Meditation*. *After Midnight: Selected Poems* is his first collection of poems.

Joseph is a Zen master and Roshi of Deep Streams Zen Institute in Santa Barbara, which offers Zen Buddhist practice, interdisciplinary education, and peace-building programs that implement new integrative models of transforming suffering. For ten years, Coming Home Project, a community service of Deep Streams Zen Institute, helped thousands of post-9/11 service members, veterans, families, and caregivers transform the unseen injuries of war. A retired psychoanalyst, Joseph now serves on the faculty of Pacifica Graduate Institute and teaches widely.

Also by Joseph Bobrow

Waking Up From War:
A Better Way Home For Veterans And Nations

ISBN 978-1-63431-034-5

Zen And Psychotherapy: Partners in Liberation

ISBN 978-0-393-70579-9

il piccolo editions is an imprint of Fisher King Enterprises.
Learn more about many other worthy publications at:
www.fisherkingpress.com